WHERE GRO\

MICHAEL BROWN

Where Grown Men Go

SALT

CROMER

PUBLISHED BY SALT PUBLISHING 2019

2 4 6 8 10 9 7 5 3 1

First published in Great Britain in 2019 by
Salt Publishing Ltd
12 Norwich Road, Cromer, Norfolk NR27 0AX United Kingdom

www.saltpublishing.com

Salt Publishing Limited Reg. No. 5293401

A CIP catalogue record for this book is available from the British Library

ISBN 978 1 78463 208 3 (Paperback edition)

Typeset in Sabon by Salt Publishing

Printed and bound in Great Britain by Clays Ltd, Elcograf S.p.A

for my father and for the girls who tolerate us

Contents

WHERE GROWN MEN GO

Figurehead

Fathers known more by absence than presence.
Closed-off rooms that wait for fathers
to unlock doors. The emptiness,

the fug of fathers' ghosts, their skin
sandpaper kiss. Men you don't want
to touch – our fathers who art

grown-up – the ones you don't know.
The silences of fathers. The keg.
The side of a chair. The close at hand.

Fathers' sudden anger. The crossword.
The half-ounce. Fathers who come and go
in the half-darks on five hours sleep.

The stained fingernails of fathers. Gone
for hours at a time. The route maps
mothballed in the head. The fastest way

from A to B. And back again. Or the most direct.
Fathers pushing the pedal to the metal
on a trunk road out of Derby.

A slick of whisky in a chipped glass.
Fathers not coming down one Christmas
in the mid-seventies. The sentences

of these fathers. The stash of words:
Swarf. Sheared. Spigot.
Fathers who spend half their lives

waiting for wives with one eye on the clock.
Fathers as strangers with broken hips.
Bits of fathers. Things fathers told

or forgot they'd said. Old anecdotes
of fathers. One quiffed soon-to-be-father
in black and white circa 1965.

Fathers who hardly believe they're fathers
but are. Fathers of sons who disappear.
The last Will and Testament of fathers.
The brooding in bed. Blocks. Gods.

Notes on a Tree

Reach for one thing beyond yourself.
Stand the test of time, rooted
to a spot. Possess nothing.

Make minims of the wind.
Weather the worst winter of a life.
Admit light. Occupy the air

to speak what we won't hear.
Exhale the dead weight of the night.
You've waited for this for years.

Hallowed

More leaving the Chelsea garden forever. More closing the wooden gate to the river. Behind him on the bank of the old world Alice and Margaret fading out. The landing stairs leading More to *all shared knowledge*. More gone from this earth. More moving from us to conscience. More reading the *small print*. More not signing the Oath of Succession. Their not knowing what to do with More or quite where to put him. More hanging round like a miasma for days at a time in a period of grace. The time of grace elapsing. Something having to be done with More. To be seen to be done with More. More taking off that cloak at Traitors' Gate. More inside thirteen feet of wall. Almost eighteen feet of floor space. His glimpsing arrow-slits of sky: *I am in good health of body, quiet of minde.* More hearing Barton hauled from her cell, tied to a hurdle – five potholed miles to hang. The first of the gang to die. More looking up from flagstone, wrapping himself in linen: *a bodie to be laide.* More in want of a haircut – in want of a wife, fearing the rack, becoming *a man without helpe.* Alice coming in the *wepynge time* calling him for a fool or a stranger she must no longer recognise: *I am become a man without help. The whole brode prison of the world.* More blessing Lady Luck for the time to make rhyme. The sadness of Christ. Words smuggled out of those walls to the crowd at Cheapside. More, now in fading light, bearing his psalter: *in this thy cell thou shalt find what abroad thou shalt too often lose.* More preparing the body. A world reformed outside. The whitewashed walls. Stolen gold and gilt, the extinguishing of all candles.

The Jamestown Brides

The first settlers were male. They could not fix
themselves or plant their puffed-out chests,

looked out west. Ate snakes. Some survived,
wrote home in want of wives to root

them to the soil. Petticoats. A promise
for a better life, they came

in rickety, half-seaworthy ships. Like this:
Orphans, maids, reckless, teenaged

girls, slips, blown off-course
to *the starving time*. They knew

their place. Those unkissed lips
harboured words, made breath.

from The Room of Common Prayer

two beakers of Campo Aldea   one untouched

a child's sing-song   remote upstairs

an empty water bottle (500 ml) on a red   white   blue black Iranian rug

unidentified birdsong   diminishing

an immaculate permafrost of window ledge dust

two   yet one   stripe of light on a far wall

a footstool

large breed dog of indeterminate stock   asleep   rhythmic breathing

an unplugged standard lamp

a dried rose   folds the colour of wine

Chalice

Something yet is kept.
You want to lift
this wrought stem, to tip the quiet freight
of its light to your lips,
its secrecies.

Feel it break. Otherness
on your tongue. Hour
and a place we have made for it.
Blood sipped. Dark released.
How might we have lived from this for so long?

My Father's Glass

It must have been miraculous for him
to hold that stem of breath. Fragile
strength blown to shape. It had to be

those last molecules of his words
that shivered from his tongue. Brittle verbs,
the urgency of a breakable love.

And his guarded heart hardly spoke of grace,
how the fluted line of glass became its freight,
his depth. A phrase he felt in fingertips.

Now I pick up this space of him to lift
or taste what's left: the giving
and downing of a life, a pledge.

The Half of It

The man came to the bed at night, he came
to the bed, the sleigh-bed his wife hadn't wanted.
He brought to the bed the softness of feathers.

The weight of a day came with him to bed.
He lay with the weather in the nest of his bones,
the man with his clothes and his pocket of coins.

He made a shape and his head was leaves
and he gave to the bed his unprotected skin,
the gravel of hurt he kept within.

Routine. A word. Sounds came in,
reached the dark scrape of him,
the bulk and the frame took everything:

his cards his cash his keys.
He was alive again in the way of sky
or dream or birds.

The Social and Economic Consequences

I found the place easily enough.
It was a Sunday and I was here to drink.
They were already six sheets to the wind.

Someone clocked me at the door,
asked if I'd ever known Gerry McConnell
or a way back from the dark
to the motorway, to the path.

A man spilled to the floor, coughed,
another might have intoned a Mass
to the brimming froth of a pint

and we had not come to think of love
as any more or less than this: a space
where grown men go to find they're lost.

Things He Needs

Bread. Milk. Blind faith.
Two front tyres.
The patience of a saint.

Light relief. Five hours'
unbroken sleep – at least.
Exercise.

Razors with two clean blades.
Tact. A full tank. Toothpaste.
The three lost tins of kidney beans

no traceable sell-by-date.
Battery life. Good grace
in defeat. Facts.

A door that shuts. ID.
A scribbled note. Keys.
Guts. Green tea.

A quiet word:
Yes – contact (with or without ties)
Time.

Our Father

I pad about the house from room to room, a sulky ghost
doing its damnedest to bed down for the night.

Noise follows me like dust. The kids have multiplied.
In the kitchen I pass through walls, softly become obsolete.

A radio is turned-up too loud. In my head I tune it out.
The dog catches my eye, seems to empathise.

A sudden shriek from the living room –
on TV someone is living life at such a pitch

where grown men don't skulk or find a place to hide
inside their own skin.

Leeds

By the awful grace of God, the people
sleep through most of Leeds, stand hardly,
half-drunk or stunned in Starbucks.

In the deep midwinter pain falls like snow
on higher ground and in the hearts
of the wise men in Weatherspoons.

Against their will comes truth, makes them
flame for a time like hope or love
in the gloom of this land.

Protocol

Though we haven't said it for a while
that ticking bomb of our word –
it felt like an abandonment
its gentle plosives richocheting
in the blue house, its bay window.
How we made its sound that raw time
between the sheets of us, to overcome
an awkwardness. Two strangers,
that invasion of another's life
or space. It was a form of words
to begin to say *It's alright*
to retreat once more
into our separate darks.
We were skin to skin back then.
You'd speak the noun
like a way to say goodbye,
a rite when everything was new,
our bodies were incense or shadow,
they had to part to form again
and you spoke out those syllables
that first night like I already knew
how this would end,
how this was the start.

Woken

The impression of not sleeping. *Not* sleeping.
The fetch of a wave held inside the head.
The thin black turning itself in, becoming sky.

A taste of lack. The ghost of your last thought.
Fibres found on your green toothbrush.
What shifts in the tissue of body. Of mind.

The pebble of a word at the back of your throat.
The tip of your tongue. The bones of the house.
What you let enter you, what possessed you.

What you let out. The thing you were thinking
 before you knew you were thinking.
The thing *itself.*

What you see in yourself. Each stroke of the heart.
The stuff, the trace. What gets under your skin.
What stays.

Stucco

Stuck on from the back-of-beyond.
A phoneme caught in the throat.
A period piece knocked through
to create bijou living space.
The architecture of vowels in the mouth.
The tongue's Italianate paste.
Relief. A render in white.
A rind to hide the grey.
The hash job to cover-up
the base and out of date.
A lie. What's gone for dust.
The hairline crack disguised.
The blind to what's out of sight,
not quite out of mind. The grate
of an old man's cough. A gunshot
going off. All shock and loss.

Loft

A photograph of you before you were you.
The inertia of furniture.

The incongruous pink of a child's doll.
The years.

A limbo of unclassified waste.
The unclaimed. A cassette tape's

intestines. The shifting weight
inside the whale. The bared

bones retained for *sentimental reasons*.
A membrane of all absences.

What's in between or kept back
held in the interstices, slats.

The space for the lost, the broken
stuff. What we thought or forgot.

A half-workable rowing machine.
A miscellany of magazines.

Where to tread carefully.
Where *not*.

A life in its lines of purchase history.
The future boxed-up. Above

what remains of us and close
to the sky. Heat rising.
A boundary we must cross.

The Soul of a Dog

That I was not body, that I was not
heart or gland or bone was a creed
only told in school, not half-believed

or known. Once I'd watched
those deep mechanics of his dog-lung breath
flinched out from that sack of skin

there was no coming back.
And when the pentobarbitone took hold
of what I used to know of him

much more than muscle closed out,
something that I'd almost laughed about,
been unable to put down.

Minor Operation

When I was four I nearly died.
My temperature sky-rocketed
fahrenheit degrees: 108, 109 . . .

I was kept alive with ice,
placed in a refrigeration tank,
my anaesthetist's last throw of the dice.

The procedure was stopped;
muscle relaxed to spasm at the brink
of being. The nick of time.

I have no memory of heat. That touch
and go limbo of dark. No photograph.
Just gaps and words adults might have said.

I don't believe in fate, how routines of days
and weeks are fixed at birth. We all pretend
we don't balance on that edge.

The Lost Saints

The renewal spread from the continent.
We called them *Saints* but really they were men,
women, too, though we hardly noticed their closeness.

All day they lived among us lettering,
healing, running with clothes
they could hardly stand up in.

They seemed to flutter out from the stations.
It went on like this: they colonised office space
and, now and then, through a dream of glass

you would glimpse a body,
harp in hand, or shaping
metal into love. Wave to pass

the time of day, you know the sort of thing.
We lost contact in the end –
those gentle souls, their sacrifice.

Annunciation

Someone arrives uninvited to tell you
what you couldn't begin to believe:

how an uneventful life might change
in an hour or with a phrase.

Receive this with grace.
Feel how the ordinary word

coils like song in the spiral of the ear;
dream's pitch, yet half-heard,

how physical, near. You can't place
that felt note, known all along,

come to earth.

Notification

As the page loads you're there again.
Icon. Friend. 36 hours offline.

In virtual space, a mind and words
I recognise in this last post you made.

And 29 likes for what's too late to say
for what has spread: that wildfire in your throat –

and all the years and all the songs are gone
and this reply I send is out of time. Wrong.

William

I suppose he was much like most men:
capable of killing and not feeling
anything. I think when I last looked at him,
his hands spilling to sky like instinct,
or at any rate the ceiling of an evening,
worn out by the ward or years
drinking tepid coffee out of boredom,
in the brash light of a clinic,
I'd just wanted to remember that river in him.

Grave Marker, Whitby Abbey

To touch a Saxon cross fine-tune your hand
to a star, arrange it to each rune with love.

Here was one who felt such slackened
feldspar through that world of stone –

eyes narrowed, intent to the fault line –
a seam of rock. Once it took such time

to score or scratch or deftly nick
these half-familiar marks where now

you strain to place your fingerprint,
to fix a dream-blade's dance,

trace the grit and grain – how the will
to rough out lives or interlace
straight lines became.

Our Deaths

Look up –
this Liverpool sky
has too long been
our lift- music
Fix this. Feel yet
the rain – its cold
slow tumble
to touch
your mouth
to come
to come to ground.
Stop thinking.

The Letters in a Girl's Name

From the outskirts of a town, say Darlington
for the sake of argument, you are perhaps
staring at the improbable satellites,
concave plates that call up and out
to an infinite space

or these backyards of a terrace block
which might yet peter-out to a park or become
the track of a man with a dog and a wife,
a scrap of land at the edge of a sky.

How you had wanted once to send such wands of light,
reach out from the dark page of yourself
to place those nine strange letters of your life.
From distance still I watch your untried hand
slur vowels, diphthongs mouthed in time
on your tongue and all the way down your right arm
to the pencil point pressed to its path,
a current to make something happen
from nothing: a name.
How you had shaped a line to call it out,
to find what it was to write, the crux
and spell of you, that first insight.

Device

That dream of a daughter's early life,
its wake of sleepless, grey mornings
to this night where I track your outbound flight

from Heathrow to St Petersburg.
You're leaving by degrees. It's alright
these days for grown men to cry

at photographs, old toys, what's left behind.
And, sometimes, when I can't sleep I rise
and in the early morning light I walk

through the bedlam of your bedroom,
to see if I might find those days
in this device I charge to bring you close.

An *App,* you'd say, if I could fetch you back
to bear what love and opened space have made.
You packed in half an hour, left this trace

and time to hold you in my hand –
a phone, this line and a man, for all his life,
tied to where you fly, where you land.

New Look

Even though the Cleveland Centre on a Sunday
possesses the indescribable sadness
we have felt thicken inside the curtains
of a photo-booth, our words rise-up
as breath from a rained-out roof-top car park.
We are here. We are, perhaps, with our kind
in some dry, humourless hour where we fidget
for the girls, the girls who tolerate us,
who gave us their times of day
and what for. Sometimes we might lose them,
acred in the minutes outside fitting-rooms.
Hardly we are fathers now. Dispersed in the numbers,
textures of us linger in lifts, glass aisles,
the fourth-storey floors where we glimpse
ourselves.
Poor, thrown things
who know that without them
we might become anyone.

NGO Documentary: Camp 722

Aya had come to the land of free movement.
Too small to roam about camp, she'd run
from the lip of the pre-fabricated world.

I'd been filming the *access to water,
sanitation, shelter.* She banged against my knee.
We spoke the lingua-franca of laughter.

Not yet 8, she ached to play. But this was war.
Unfazed, I gave her the gift of my shades
and the evil eye. It was only later

when I'd got away, I'd remember Greece,
Eid Mubarak and that broken lens
through which I'd watched

the borders of us blur
to one rootless earth.

Sarah's Character

If the depth of love is measured by its loss
like the lazy half-formed way you made an S
that once to mark the margin of my page

and since for years it's kept its place, this glyph,
your trace in shape and dark and raw,
let's leave its composition in the book –

a letter I can't yet write out
or look at anymore.

Sheffield

When you arrive it is *far*.
In the wrong city the snow falls
like little shocks of other –
your knee-length coat
flapping open –

all day the buses move about the mid-eighties
in cream and brown, they stall at suburbs
with their tremendous and groundless names:
Intake, Herdings, Dore.

A dark afternoon. You find yourself
alone on the sixth floor of Sorby Hall –
a compass needle whirring in your heart.

Effects

A roadmap opened on the London Orbital.
A Styrofoam cup. A phone box
six miles east of Peterborough.
One receipt for unleaded fuel.
A multi-pack of hard-boiled sweets.
A scribbled note of an address of a bedsit
in some affordable street.
The code for Leeds.
An empty passenger seat.
Three plastic bags filled to the brim
with what he's got, doesn't need.

Boundary

Start with the sky. Its possibility.
For the first time in a life,
touch the right side of a face.
And who can ever cross or close
a divide such as this ?
This river's half-mile, its slur of light?
We elide. Time slips away without us.
Above Birkenhead the cloud fells break,
open us to endless blue
and we are blind.

Crossing

Days like these when the mediocre light
hardly makes us look up for music,
we might still be ourselves. Remember
the furious quiet off Mull when we thought
we were listening to the thin sky break
– that place in the open skin of the sky –
for something spoken, out of range.

The Way

I drive the five and a half miles from home
to work and it is as if the interim
was another life. I cross a bridge

and what is right *there* in front of my eyes:
cars, the italic dance of birds, red and green
light, a waxing moon –

such sights might make another man
realise how it was the way
he arrived.

Lines

Your father's dying breed (maternal side).
Ravel of Mersey's coil and arch to sea.
The crow's feet radiating from your half-closed eyes.
A memory of a woman's waist.
That stitch in time. The broken,
dotted, contoured either side
of *between*. Those that remain
right smack in the crosshairs of the sights.
The stroke. The slash.
The route and track. The zig-zag. The night
as surely follows day and all the way back
to the crack of doom. Pylons seen
in a rear view mirror. Your life and love
in the palm of your hand.
The towing of. The bringing into.
The border. The path. The marks,
the marks on a map and drawn in sand.

Rear-View Mirror

And the more you drive a road the quicker
the journey and things receding into the familiar
were once astonishing. Must you spell it out
like the notes that are not notes but the joy
the blackbird sings in the half-dark, the catch
in your throat when you see someone else,
that ghost in the green-grey eyes of a face
you think you've known all your life.

Threshold

November's thrum of rain in knock-off scraps of England,
the punctuated, joyless yap of a tied-up terrier
or, then again, that permanent ocean-note of traffic
two miles away on the A19 south of Teesside.
These shy tones are all you know of silence.
But this is not silence.
And if you ever lost or forgot
these waves, you would be someone else,
their ear cupped lightly to catch
the chambered echo of a half-remembered song,
out of range now, not quite gone –

North Sea, Redcar: Mechanical Failure

More alive it seems than you, than me,
this place – such womb-notes fetched from deep,
its remembered pitch.

Across the front passenger seat
I reach out a hand
for your wound-down window, touch
instead the space of a heart,
that gentle *lub dub*,
something dark.

Coastal Retreat

after Frances Cornford

Far-off gulls like risen souls at high tide.
What we found was the lost cause of soft chalk,
drowned cows, half a house at the edge of life.

They knew mudflats no more than calving ice.
They stood their ground on salt marsh and bedrock.
Far-off gulls like risen souls at high tide.

What moves on or leaves in time is what survives.
What resists or believes too late is caught.
Drowned cows, half a house at the edge of life.

They built dykes on sand, watched the waves subside,
evolved from sea to land and learned to walk
or fly like gulls, like risen souls at high tide.

Off a spit from a stack they recognise
the grey shale of days, one unforeseen shock.
Drowned cows, half a house at the edge of life.

In five weeks we'd make out a hillside,
the spire's striptease, the stopped hands of its clock.
Far off gulls like risen souls at high tide.
Drowned cows, half a house at the edge of life.

Deny

Six miles under the sea-bed plates shift.

This time it's not quite enough

to make half a continent slip

off the map.

Things realign.

And we might exist like this for days,

weeks from the first tantrum of that wave,

hardly daring ourselves to breathe.

Trace

Long after we'd been wiped off the face of the map
they met us in micro-plastic waves, bits,
remains of bigger things –
as the letters of a Roman stone degrade
to earth or a polystyrene sea
comes back with its phrase of beads,
the spiked diet of birds.

The Years

Because we could not reach the sea that day
we learned to imagine what could not be felt:
how our river's sluggish course drew wind,
salt's graze and became something else.

And how we knew it would not be the same
when some restless force
brought us like waves to the coast
to change like spray and swell and sound.

Notes on Waves

To have children, to grow old creeps up in increments.
We can't see this, of course, in the days and the days that fall
like stones. We are too close.

Shifting, tiring, we come to the place. There's nothing
changed from how it once seemed. The sea has not moved.
Our bodies hardly bear what they held.

The energy makes landfall and breaks to sound.
It doesn't know what to do with itself.

Water Lilies

We are watching the sun's slow dive
into the Wirral. You want to touch
the water-stars of its last light.
Soon it will be time for us
to separate.

Outside this frame of hush
that weightless walk back
from the Tate –
where I had wanted to fall
inside the green water lilies
that lay like time
or surface tension.
Do you remember them –
caught in paint,
their lawlessness of oil?

And here a ferry from Ireland
skulks home to Birkenhead,
its gentle wake of damage
some force fetched to land.

Welcome to Liverpool

I want you to stay
like this. In the time
that remains before the train –
I must hold, hold this.

Golden Gate

Some say that those who fall,
who let go to find thin air or nothing at all
but their own dead weight
between themselves and earth,
survive five vast seconds of time
to grasp they've changed their minds
before the final impact.
How that voice in their head has gone –
and all there is now is just this wish
to hold on.

Acknowledgements

I am grateful to John Glenday for his thoughtful advice over the years. I would also like to thank Paul Stephenson for his encouragement. I am grateful to New Writing North for a New North Poets Award in 2017. My thanks also to Colette Bryce, Clare Pollard, Maria Isakova Bennett, Carole Bromley, Judy Brown and Ben Wilkinson. I am also grateful to Heather, Genevieve and Philippa for their constant supply of raw material.

Acknowledgements are also due to the editors of the following publications: *Southword*, *Crannog* and *The North* in which some of these poems first appeared. 'Figurehead' won first prize in the 2018 Wirral Festival of Firsts Poetry Competition, 'Water Lilies' won third prize in the York Poetry Competition 2015 and 'Hallowed' won second Prize in York Poetry Competition 2019.

NEW POETRY FROM SALT

AMIT CHAUDHURI
Sweet Shop (978-1-78463-182-6)

DAVID BRIGGS
Cracked Skull Cinema (978-1-78463-207-6)

PETER DANIELS
My Tin Watermelon (978-1-78463-209-0)

MATTHEW HAIGH
Death Magazine (978-1-78463-206-9)

ANDREW MCDONNELL
The Somnambulist Cookbook (978-1-78463-199-4)

ELEANOR REES
The Well at Winter Solstice (978-1-78463-184-0)

TONY WILLIAMS
Hawthorn City (978-1-78463-212-0)

This book has been typeset by
SALT PUBLISHING LIMITED
using Sabon, a font designed by Jan Tschichold
for the D. Stempel AG, Linotype and Monotype Foundries.
It is manufactured using Holmen Book Cream 70gsm,
a Forest Stewardship Council™ certified paper from the
Hallsta Paper Mill in Sweden. It was printed and bound
by Clays Limited in Bungay, Suffolk, Great Britain.

CROMER
GREAT BRITAIN
MMXIX